The Quakers in Chichester

1655 - 1967

Third (Tercentenary) Edition

The Religious Society of Friends
Chichester Meeting

PREFACE

This brief history would have been impossible without the extensive and scholarly researches of Eric Millington. His notes and papers, together with some of my own, are now in the care of the Preparative Meeting librarian for the benefit of future historians. Thanks are due to the many people who have given time and help but particularly to Dr Spencer Thomas for his research on the history of John Barton Hack, Ruthellen Davis for her work in Pennsylvania, and Humphrey Tranter, Clerk of the Adelaide Meeting.

MW 1999

First published 1998
Second edition 1999
Third edition 2000

Published by: The Religious Society of Friends, Chichester Meeting

ISBN 0 9534828 0 4

Cover picture: The Priory Road Meeting House 1700-1967

1: Seekers and Radicals

On a Saturday in the late summer of 1655 a strange little group made its way from Arundel into Chichester. They almost certainly approached the town down the street called St Pancras which led to one of the city's still standing gates. Most of the buildings both in the street and in Eastgate Square had been flattened in the Civil War thirteen years earlier, and apart from a little row of newly built cottages adjoining the site of St Pancras church, there would have been a clear view of the city walls.

There were at least two travellers, quite possibly more. The leader was a 31 year old roaming preacher called George Fox, an eccentric and difficult man. His way of dressing may well have attracted attention as the group entered the town as it was very distinctive: for many years he was given to wearing a leather suit and an extremely large hat. His hair was unfashionably long and, though he avoided any hint of Royalist colour or finery, even the Puritans (the Royalists' greatest enemies) thought his appearance rather odd.

Fox was no figure of fun though: he had great presence, and some would suggest that despite his strange appearance he was very attractive, his strong personality giving him a dangerous magnetism. Several of the people who met him wrote of his amazing eyes. In a superstitious age there were those who associated his penetrating gaze with witchcraft, a capital crime at the time, though not one of which he was ever formally accused. It is unlikely that he had been an easy travelling companion on the road from Arundel, as he was given to impenetrable silences interspersed with passionate and sometimes lengthy outbursts. But it must also be said that he inspired tremendous loyalty - the other known traveller, for instance, as he entered Chichester that day, was Ambrose Rigge, a young man of twenty or twenty one who had left home just to follow him. Fox was an inspirational character, sometimes drawing crowds of hundreds to hear him preach. His message was outspoken and uncompromising and as a result he was familiar with the inside of various prisons. Yet the last time he had been inside one, in the spring of that same year, he had been sent to meet Cromwell himself, and had, moreover, been given his liberty by the Lord Protector. In short he was a powerful and highly complex person who, despite his humble origins, and his remarkable ability to annoy people, was a national character.

Passing through the East Gate the travellers would have found themselves in East Street, but a rather different looking street from that of today as the great building boom of the early eighteenth century had not yet given Chichester its characteristic Georgian appearance. The houses and shops were still timber framed and many had top floors which jutted out over the roadway in the Tudor fashion. At number 21, on the corner of St Andrew's Court, they would have passed the house of William Cawley, the local MP, the man who had captured the town for Parliament, assembling his forces on the Broyle fields just to the north of where the Festival Theatre stands today. Cawley is chiefly remembered as one of those who sat in the High Court which condemned Charles I. Indeed he was one of those who signed the death warrant. Later, after the monarchy had been restored, loyal Cicestrians erected a bust of the unfortunate Charles in the market cross, on the east side, looking sternly down the road at the house in which his tormentor had lived.

Fox was 'religious' and Cawley 'political' but were both products of the Reformation, an extraordinary period of ecclesiastical and cultural revolution which had been going on for the previous hundred and twenty years. Henry VIII had made the initial break with Rome, instituted some overdue reforms (of church finance for example) but had otherwise been something of a reconciler, trying to keep the country united and his 'high church' and 'low church' citizens all within a single Church of England. Edward VI, who followed him, was much more decisively Protestant, and his commissioners ruthlessly stripped churches of their and the nation's artistic heritage. Crucifixes were pulled down, statues defaced and paintings destroyed. Chichester Cathedral still bears the marks of their depredations. However one great artistic monument did emerge from this period - Archbishop Cranmer's 1549 prayer-book.

Seekers and Radicals

After King Edward came Queen Mary and under her the country reverted to Catholicism, land previously taken from the 'high' bishops was restored to them, and Cranmer was burnt at the stake in Oxford. Even here in Chichester there were two unfortunates burnt in the cathedral precincts, Thomas Iveson and Richard Hook. Little is known of Hook but Iveson was a carpenter arrested with two others for reading the Bible in English. Urged to recant, he refused to do so and was martyred on 24th July 1555, just a hundred years before the visit of Fox.

Elizabeth, who took the throne in 1558, was like her father Henry, monarch for around forty years, and like him she wanted her church to be all things to almost all men. This was a policy she pursued with such skill that while the English church turned 'low' again, and the 'high' bishops lost their estates again, and the country filled up with returning Protestant exiles, she was not finally excommunicated by the Pope until twelve years after her accession.

These great shifts and swings in ecclesiastical policy were to continue. The Catholics made an attempt on the life of King James in 1605, the Gunpowder Plot, while his son King Charles was so ill thought of by the Puritans that when the country was riven by civil war, in 1642, one of the primary aims of Parliament was to make the country safe for Protestantism.

It was from this ferment that Quaker beliefs and Fox, their greatest early exponent, were to spring. The same thoughts were occuring to different people in different parts of the country. In 1646, Oliver Cromwell, not yet more than a soldier, had voiced an interesting idea, "To be a Seeker is the next best sect to a Finder, and such shall every faithful humble Seeker be at the end". Independently of Cromwell a group of open-minded searchers for truth, the Children of Light, emerged in Nottinghamshire in 1648, and elsewhere adherents of a similar movement were known as the Westmorland Seekers. For over a hundred years different groups of Christians had been proclaiming so many, sometimes irreconcilable, truths, that seeking, in humble and faithful fashion, was an appealing notion to many people. It was an idea whose time had come, and in Fox the various seekers found a

A

JOURNAL,

OR

Historical Account

OF THE

Life, Travels, Sufferings,

And CHRISTIAN

EXPERIENCES, &c.

OF

GEORGE FOX.

We passed on to one *Thomas Pachin*'s, where we had a Meeting, unto which several *Friends* came from *London*; and *John Bolton* and his *Wife* came thither on *foot* in *frost* and *snow*. After we had parted with *Friends* there, we went towards *Horsham-park*; and having visited *Friends* there, we passed on to *Arundel* and *Chichester*, where we had *Meetings*. At *Chichester* many *Professors* came in, and some *jangling* they made; but the *Lord*'s *Power* was over them. The *Woman* of the *House*, where the *Meeting* was, though she was *Convinced* of *Truth*, yet not keeping her Mind close to that which *Convinced* her; she fell in *love* with a *man* of the *World*, that was there that time. When I knew it, I took her aside, and was moved to *speak* to her, and to *pray* for her: But a *light thing* got up in her Mind, and she slighted it. Afterwards she *Married* that *man*; and soon after went *distracted*: for the Man was greatly in *Debt*, and she greatly *disappointed*. Then was I sent for to her; and the *Lord* was intreated, and *Raised her up* again, and settled her *Mind* by his *Power*.

Horsham-park. Arundel. Chicester.

Extracts from the 1694 edition of George Fox's Journal owned by the Meeting.

voice and a leader. This was the man who came into Chichester that Saturday afternoon in 1655.

That night he and his people stayed at a woman's house, probably that of Margery Wilkinson who lived on the site of what is today 62/3 North Street. A meeting was held in the house and Fox was to write later in his Journal that "... many professors came in and some janglings there were, but the Lord's power was over all" which is to say there were a lot of believers, some disturbance, but that it was a worthwhile and reverent meeting. He goes on to recount how the woman of the house was "convinced", but was in love with a man, also present at the meeting, whom she later married, and then discovered to be a bad lot. She was, in the Journal's words "greatly distracted", but later returned to Quaker ways, meeting Fox on at least two further occasions, both before and after she was widowed. The reason for thinking this woman might have been Margery Wilkinson is that she, Margery, was later prominent in the Chichester Meeting, indeed the Sunday meetings for worship were held in her house in 1669. She was also a widow by that time. It is not specifically recorded that Fox ever visited Chichester again, but he did travel in Sussex in 1657, visiting friends, and also in 1668, so they may have met each other again on those occasions.

The account in the Journal is supplemented by that of Ambrose Rigge who records that the next morning, Sunday, Fox went to the Baptist meeting, at that time held in a house in South Street. He was "listened to for a while but at length taken by the constable before the Mayor." This strongly suggests that he spoke without invitation, interrupting the service (something he was very prone to do) until the embarrassed Baptists had him hauled away.

The story gets more revealing, for the Mayor, one Richard Manning, fell in a rage with him for not taking off his hat, a normal courtesy in the seventeenth century. Fox refused to take off his hat to anyone, and frequently got into trouble as a result. He insisted that all men should be treated with equal respect as all "had that of God in them". He also insisted on always using the familiar second person singular, 'thee/thou', rather than the more respectful 'you', for the same egalitarian reasons. The revolution which had led to the King's execution had opened men's eyes to the possibility of a less hierarchical world. The egalitarianism of Fox reflected the ideas of the period: the Levellers, for example, were adherents of a popular democratic movement which insisted that authority should only be wielded with the consent of the people - an elected Parliament should be sovereign, its power only qualified by a respect for basic human rights. The equality of men was another idea whose time had come during the Civil War and it was an idea which greatly influenced George Fox and his followers.

His refusal to doff his cap to the Mayor of Chichester, or anyone else, was widely copied by other Quakers: there is a story told of the high-born William Penn who, many years later, on being received for an audience with Charles II, was surprised to see the King remove his own headgear. "Why dost thou take off thy hat, Friend Charles?" he is supposed to have asked. "It is the custom of this place that only one man should go hatted at a time" replied the King urbanely.

It seems the Mayor of Chichester was not quite so urbane in his dealings with Fox though he did let him go, apparently unconvinced by the accusation that the man was a Jesuit. This accusation was not uncommon at the time, there being much paranoia about disguised Catholics fomenting revolution. The situation was not helped by Quaker refusal to swear the Oath of Allegiance which had been introduced after the gunpowder plot, supposedly to ensure that all Catholics were loyal citizens. The problem for Quakers was that they refused to swear any oaths (and still do incidentally), on the basis of New Testament teaching - let your yea be yea, and your nay be nay. It must be assumed that the Oath was not tendered at Fox's appearance in the Chichester Court for he would most certainly have declined it and been imprisoned. As it was he was allowed to go, having been searched, and two days later left for the West of England.

So began the Quaker, or Friends' Meeting in the town. (The official name is The Religious Society of Friends, but the word Quaker is much used and was even incorporated into early Acts of Parliament). Records of the meeting are sparse in those early years but some do

Chichester City

1658 James Larbee for goeing into the high Steeple house of ye
Citty of Chichester and Speaking to the preist: Speed —
Conserning false doctrin delivered by him: was by
the magists of the place Committed to prison into the
hands of a Cruill Keeper: Ed: Lean where he Suffd:
near 5 months: and dyed within few: dayes and after he was
Set free Severall brooses that he Receaved in his Body
Remained till the day of his death wittness Wm & prudence
Clayton

Chichester City

1658 James Larbol for going into the high steeple house of ye City of Chichester and speaking to the priest (Speed) concerning false doctrine delivered by him: was by the magistrates of the place committed to prison into the hands of a gaol keeper (Edward Lean) where he suffered near 5 months and died within a few days after he was set free. Several bruises that he received on his body remained till the day of his death. Witnesses Wm & Prudence Clayton

exist. In 1658 an early member, James Larbel, went into the high steeplehouse (the Cathedral) took issue with the priest for preaching false doctrine, and was arraigned before the magistrate. He was sent to prison and suffered for five months at the hands of the gaoler Edward Lean. He died a few days after his release still bearing several bruises from the beatings he had received. Joanne, his wife, died the following year and was buried with him in Whyke churchyard.

There were other burials, a sad case of a different kind being that of Jeane Smith, John Smith's daughter, in 1661, followed shortly after by her mother Grace. They were buried in St Andrews, now the Centre of Arts but then the parish church of William Cawley. John Smith was a prominent member seven years later in 1668 - the Meeting was being held in his house in the Hornet (somewhere between the Eastgate and Bush Inns). He married his second wife, Priscilla, in the same year. Earlier, in 1663, Timothy Hale had written his will, appointing his body to be buried at the discretion of Friends in his "herb garden at Easthampnett, at the east end thereof" where his grave would catch the afternoon sun. He left bequests to named members and five pounds for "those that labour in the Word" (travelling preachers like Fox) and another five pounds for "poor Friends belonging to the Meeting". In 1664 William Clayton of Whyke (who had testified to Larbel's suffering) was imprisoned for six months for attending a Quaker meeting. The first formal record of a Meeting in Chichester was in 1668, but there clearly was one before that, albeit without all the records which later became a feature of Quaker life. Friends became very careful to record marriages, for instance, to avoid any accusation of impropriety in relationships which were not strictly legal.

2: Suspected of Sedition 1660:1700

During the ten years following George Fox's first visit there were dramatic changes in government which were to have a profound effects on all Quakers. Cromwell died in 1658 and after two years of uncertainty Charles II was invited to return from exile and assume the crown. Charles had smoothed the way to his return by issuing the Declaration of Breda promising a general amnesty, respect for Parliament and religious toleration. The amnesty, known as the Act of Oblivion, was duly passed, the only exceptions being people involved in the execution of his father. William Cawley was exiled to the Continent, never returned to Chichester, and never saw the bust of Charles I glaring down the street at his front door.

Charles II kept his promises to Parliament but Parliament itself, now filled with distrustful Royalists, made religious toleration impossible. The Quakers were seen as radical Puritans and quite possibly seditious. The country seethed with plots and rumours of plots. It was only twelve years since the horrors of the Civil War and the execution of the last King, so men who refused to take oaths, wouldn't pay tithes, insisted on wearing their hats, and spoke to their betters in the familiar thee/thou form were promptly singled out for retribution. No matter that one of their number, Margaret Fell, presented to King and Parliament the Peace Testimony which was to become a classic part of Friends' tradition. "We are a people that follow after those things that make for peace, love and unity...(We) do deny and bear our testimony against all strife and wars and contentions". Parliament was unconvinced: the Friends had too much in common with the Levellers – men who had actively fomented mutiny.

The Quaker Act of 1662 was one of the series of measures curtailing religious liberty known collectively as the Clarendon Code. It became illegal to refuse an oath, and illegal for five or more Quakers to assemble for worship. The Meeting in Arundel was raided and the members brought to Chichester to be sentenced. They were hobbled together in chains and paraded down the main streets to the gaol above the East Gate where they were treated very brutally by the gaoler. Gaolers at the time made their living by charging the prisoners for their keep - the Arundel men were asked a groat a night - and Friends who wouldn't pay as a form of protest were harshly treated. Two of their number, Nicholas Rickman and Edward Hamper, were separated from the rest and "thrown in withthe felons" rather than being kept in the relevant comfort of the jailkeeper's house.

The East Gate looking into East Street 1782. The gaol was in the rooms over the gate.

Another of the early victims of the legislation against holding meetings was the young William Penn (later the founder of Pennsylvania) who was sent down from Oxford for attending a Quaker meeting. The response of Chichester Friends to the oppression is not known but elsewhere in the country valiant stands were taken and Quakers continued to meet in public despite the widespread attacks and imprisonments. They refused either to conceal their meetings or to respond to taunts other than by turning the cheek. This combination of straightforwardness and non-aggression in the face of persecution won them considerable sympathy and within months the King had ordered the release of all but the ringleaders. In 1668 much of the legislation expired and was not replaced for another two years, and then with less repressive measures.

It was in 1668 that an organisational structure was decided upon for the emerging sect. Local Meetings were grouped together geographically and met once a month in administrative sessions called, very logically, Monthly Meetings. Chichester was part of the Chichester and Arundel Monthly Meeting which also included Steyning (just north of Worthing), Petworth, and Birdham. The latter was a short lived assembly of some twenty or thirty people which met in the house of one Richard Green who with his wife got into trouble with the authorities for wilfully absenting himself from his parish church, a legal offence.

On the sixth of October the first Monthly Meeting was held in Arundel, and it was not a happy day for Chichester. It is minuted that arrangements were put in hand for two respected Friends from other parts of the county to visit the Cathedral City and "exhort all those who have dishonoured God in the Meeting". There is no indication as to exactly what form the dishonour had taken. The reproof would have been delivered "in the high red house of John Smith in St Pancras," the parish not the street, for John Smith lived in the Hornet. The minute, incidentally, is dated 6th Day of the 8th Month. This Quaker form of dating was an eccentricity at the time, avoiding any reference to heathen gods long before the rest of the world started using all figure dates. Before the reform of the English calendar the year began in March so the eighth month was October. Friends also numbered weekdays from one to seven, the First Day being Sunday.

First Day meetings in 1669 were being held at Margery Wilkinson's house in North Street where, on the 6th July Chichester's third Quaker marriage took place between Joshua Kirck of Leadenhall in London and Margaret Reynolds. Nothing more is heard of this couple who presumably went to live at Joshua's house in London. Margery

Wilkinson though appears in the records again three years later when, together with Richard Green, Edward Hamper and others, she leased a piece of land in the Hornet for use as a burial ground. It was a thousand year lease and the burial ground is still there, now a Quaker freehold, and let to the District Council as a small garden.

Edward Hamper was one of those who had been thrown in with the felons in the East Gate gaol. He was a man of property and after this experience he created, in 1675, an unusual legal trust to protect his estate from seizure. His Arundel houses were made over to Quaker trustees in return for a modest annual income. There were many trustees, each of whom could act alone, so that if the Meeting were raided there was a reasonable chance that someone would still be available to manage the estate. This precaution was not of immediate use, as life became a little easier for Dissenters during the 1670s. Laws were amended and a Declaration of Indulgence made by the King. There were still some problems though, as in 1678 when William Cooper of Whyke was accused by the church wardens of having Quaker meetings in his house.

Sussex Quarterly Meeting requested Ambrose Galloway, a draper from Lewes, to collect information from Friends about their sufferings. He recorded them year by year starting back in 1655 listing fines and imprisonments. Chichester members such as James Larbel and William Clayton suffered imprisonment in those early years of legal persecution, and there was an unusual extra-legal challenge in Bishop Peter Gunning, who was appointed to the see in 1670. This man was so ardent that he is reported to have disturbed dissenting meetings in person, but he does not seem to have been vicious. Indeed, unusually for the age, he gave a public challenge to Quakers, Presbyterians and Baptists and appointed three days for disputation in the Cathedral.

Disputation of another kind took place in the courts, in London, where William Penn was charged with attending the Gracechurch Street Meeting. The jury refused to find him guilty despite being dreadfully bullied by the judge who twice sent them away, without food or other comforts, to reconsider their verdict. After three days of this the judge imprisoned them all, for contempt of court. A considerable legal struggle ensued but finally the point was won and the rights of an English jury established.

A few years later Penn inherited considerable property in Sussex and came to make his home at Warminghurst near Pulborough. It is probable that he visited Chichester, the county town and only twenty miles away, though there is no actual record of his having done so. The Chichester Meeting would certainly have had regular contact with Warminghurst, which was to be an important Quaker centre for the thirty one years that it was home to Penn. In 1677, for example, after the London Yearly Meeting, he entertained the Quaker leaders George Fox and Robert Barclay. The authorities came to hear that illegal religious meetings were being held in the house and those present expected to be raided by the militia. In an act of open defiance a huge open air meeting was arranged, several hundred Friends attended, probably including some from Chichester. There was great tension but in the event they were undisturbed.

William Penn was not only an effective leader but also a prolific writer. Pepys, was surprised by his book on the Trinity. "I got my wife to read it to me and I find it so well writ as I think it too good for him ever to have writ it - and it is a serious sort of book and not fit for everybody to read." One of the first guests at Warminghurst was another thinker and writer, Robert Barclay whose 'Apology' is a Quaker classic, asserting that no man could be regarded as excluded from salvation: a doctrine of inclusivity. The idea was very different from that of the Presbyterians, for example, who at the time were fiercely pre-destinationist, believing that only the elect could find grace. The Puritans had devised tests to make their churches companies of people each of whom was destined for 'salvation'. The Quakers avoided both tests and sacraments: no humble faithful seeker was excluded. Much was borrowed from Puritan Christianity, plain meeting houses and transparent honesty for example. But much was different - the unprogrammed meetings, where anyone could speak if so moved, (as is still the case today) and, most importantly, that there was no prescription for salvation, just companionship on the road thereto.

For Chichester Friends the road was to become somewhat bumpy in the following years. They had at last, shortly after Penn's great meeting, rented themselves a building for worship. It was on the far side of the burial ground in the Hornet, right on the edge of the town, adjoining the field used as a cattle pound. Then in 1683 came the Rye House Plot. Some prominent Whigs were uncovered in a plot to assassinate the King, and in the hiatus which followed the Tories were in the ascendent, and determined to control any potential trouble-makers. A great new wave of religious persecution swept the country. In Chichester this was to reach a climax in July and then to continue unabated till October. The suffering was graphically recorded at the time: "...Friends belonging to Chichester Meeting being met together at their usual meeting place at or near Chichester, the soldiers then quartered at Chichester came in amongst them and violently broke the glass windows of the house and the tables forms and benches all to pieces and were so rude and abusive to the women Friends that they could no more than keep themselves from their beastly designs on them ... but it pleased the Lord in wonderful manner to preserve them without the mischief on their persons" Frustrated in their attacks on the women the soldiers dragged the whole assembly out of the place by force.

The Meeting had been denounced by informers, and because of the information laid by them warrants for distress were granted against attenders. These warrants were an early form of fine, paid in goods rather than cash. A poor smith, the Richard Green from Birdham who had previously been in trouble for not attending his parish church and who now attended the Chichester Meeting, lost two hogs, his bed, bedding, vice, sledges and iron, in all worth four pounds ten shillings. The informers returned repeatedly, often drunk, and accompanied by soldiers. The following account has all the marks of being dictated by a group of people all chiming in excitedly with their own points and memories. The clerk who recorded it was so harassed that he failed to include any full stops.

"They were constant abusers of the innocent, they several times broke the windows of the house and the doors, and the door of the

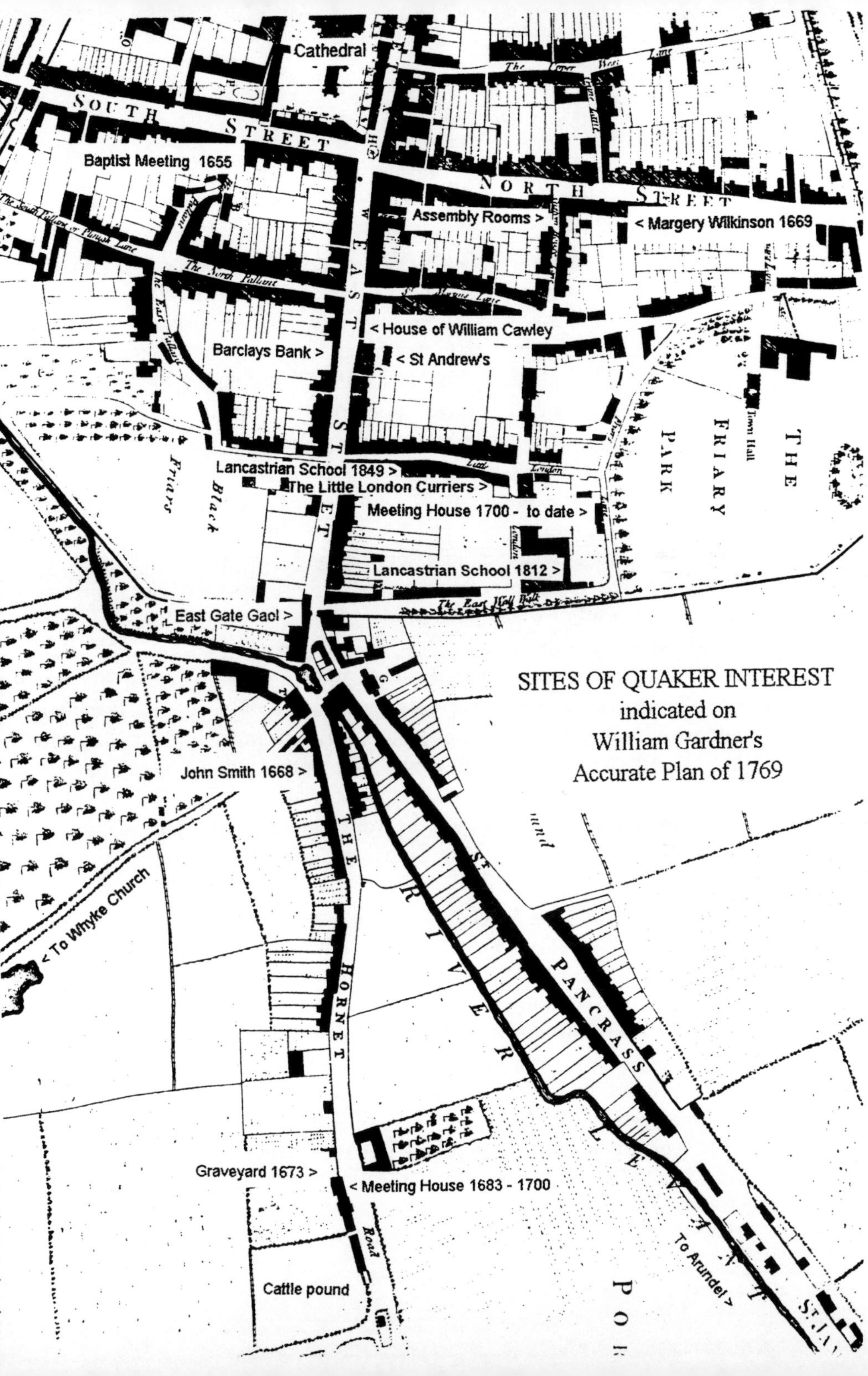
SITES OF QUAKER INTEREST
indicated on
William Gardner's
Accurate Plan of 1769
Cathedral
SOUTH STREET
NORTH STREET
EAST ST
Baptist Meeting 1655
Assembly Rooms >
< Margery Wilkinson 1669
< House of William Cawley
Barclays Bank >
< St Andrew's
Lancastrian School 1849 >
The Little London Curriers >
Meeting House 1700 - to date >
Lancastrian School 1812 >
East Gate Gaol >
John Smith 1668 >
< To Whyke Church
THE HORNET
ST PANCRASS
RIVER
Graveyard 1673 >
< Meeting House 1683 - 1700
Cattle pound
To Arundel >
THE FRIARY PARK
Black Friars
Town Hall

burying ground, and laid the burying ground open to the highway and burned the fence which was about it, and as often as Friends made any small reparations of anything they came and destroyed all, the following meeting, and stuffed up the meeting house doorplace, having before carried away the door, with bushes and thrust the bushes against Friends' legs, and tore a Friend's scarf from her neck and bid Friends complain to the justices if they would, and if any small matter for seats was provided by laying a few bricks and loose boards on them, they came and broke all to pieces, and threw a serpent, as they call it, composed of powder etc (a kind of firework) into the meeting which was like to have done mischief, being a thatched house, and affrighted the children at the meeting, and all this performed with great swearing and threatening and chiefly enacted by the two informers who were commonly drunk when in this service, and sometimes accompanied with the rabble of rude boys and others, the informers telling Friends that if they would be obedient to the King's laws and come to church etc all would be well."

It was too much for Margery Wilkinson who went off and complained first to the Bishop's Chancellor, (a senior legal officer) and then to the magistrates. She got short shrift from them. They told her that Friends were meeting illegally and nothing could be done. The attendant constable gave an old fashioned warning about the law taking its full course if any more were heard. In the case of Henry Dixon the law took a terrible course - the Chichester court sent him to gaol where he died three months later. The oppression was not to last much longer though: in 1685 King Charles died, James II came to the throne, and the political atmosphere changed for the better.

In 1681, two or three years before these events, Charles II had settled a long-standing debt to the Penn family by licensing the territory then known as West Jersey (in America) to William. The King wanted the new colony renamed in honour of William's father, Admiral Penn, and given the wooded countryside there, the title Pennsylvania was decided upon. In 1682 William left Warminghurst for the New World with about a hundred Friends, many from Sussex, mainly from the Horsham Monthly Meeting but some perhaps from

Chichester. He was one of only a very few colonial proprietors of his day to visit America.

There were already a few Quaker settlers in the new colony when Penn and his group arrived. William Clayton and his family from Chichester had moved there in 1677. Clayton was a carpenter from the suburb of Whyke who had witnessed the suffering of James Larbol in 1658 (page 7) and been imprisoned himself in 1664. The family undoubtedly knew Penn from their days in Sussex where Clayton had been treasurer of the Monthly Meeting and active in Quarterly Meeting affairs. In 1682 he sold Penn 206 acres of what is now central Philadelphia, and in 1683 he was elected to the Council where he took an active part on the committee that revised the Frame of Government of the colony. The family, with other Friends, established a township a few miles to the west of Philadelphia and called it, nostalgically, Chichester. Early meetings for worship were held in members' homes.

The liberal constitution which Penn, Clayton and the Friends wrote for the Quaker state was in many ways ahead of its time. Peaceable relations were established with the Native American communities, there was religious freedom for all, the death penalty all but abolished. Oaths and military spending were both excluded from law and government. Slavery was not abolished but slaves were guaranteed their freedom after a certain period of service. A few years later Penn was to suggest another idea ahead of its time - a union of the American colonies. When this was finally achieved a hundred years later, and independence gained, the constitution of the new United States was much influenced by that of Pennsylvania.

Penn himself did not stay long in the colony he had so helped to establish but returned to his family in Sussex two years later, landing at Worthing in 1684. Perhaps it was Penn who carried back the cheerful letter from William Clayton dated 1683: "We have no cause to mourn. Our lot is fallen every day in a goodly place, and the love of God is growing among us, and .... truly great is our joy therefor."

In England the times were not so happy. Edward Hamper died in Horsham gaol in 1684 having been arrested again the previous year, at the time when Chichester Friends suffered so much. Hamper was a shoemaker in Arundel and comfortably off: in addition to his Trust, which became a Quaker Charity on his death, he left money to many members of his family and also his old friend Ambrose Rigge, the man who had travelled to Chichester with George Fox thirty years before. Among his family was included his cousin John Martin, a member of the Chichester Meeting. Hamper seems to have had close ties with Chichester for he also left money to some members to whom he was not related including both Richard Green and Margery Wilkinson, who each received twenty shillings. A further five pounds was left to Margery and John Hammond jointly "to be of their disposing about their meeting house", a useful bequest after the damage caused by the soldiers, informers and 'rude boys'. Shortly after, perhaps because of the problems which Friends' occupation of the building had provoked, the landlord decided to sell it. The 1687 freehold was in three names, John Martin, John Hammond and the trustees of the Quarterly Meeting. This complicated arrangement was to cause problems later.

One problem of which Friends were to be relieved was that of persecution, for with the accession of William and Mary there came the Toleration Act which ended most of the penalties for religious dissent (though it left the Clarendon laws on the statute book). This reform was passed just in time for George Fox and Robert Barclay to see it: Barclay died in 1690, Fox in 1691, the first generation of Friends was ending. The death of Fox was marked by a letter from the London Yearly Meeting testifying, as is the Quaker custom, to "the grace of God as shown in his life." One of the signatories was Ambrose Rigge, the then young man who had accompanied Fox when he first came to Chichester in 1655. Margery Wilkinson fades from the record in the 1680s but as her death is nowhere recorded she perhaps went to spend her old age away from the town. A death which was recorded was that of James Lucas in December 1693. He was a very prosperous carpenter who earlier the same year had leased a site in Eastgate which had stood empty since the Civil War. Then he was taken ill and by November was so sick that he made his will, providing generously for his five young children, his loving wife Ann and his mother Joanne. He also left the impressive sum of forty pounds to "his friends called Quakers to buy or build a meeting house to meet in to worship God". In those days such a sum was sufficient to buy a small building - it was largely because of the generosity of Lucas that Friends were eventually able to move to the Priory Road site.

William Penn, who was living in Warminghurst at the time, would certainly have heard about this dramatic development in Chichester. He was virtually under house arrest in 1693 for though repression was slowly easing it was not yet entirely over. He occupied himself writing a short treatise entitled "An essay towards the present and future peace of Europe by the establishment of a European Parliament". The next year Penn was completely acquitted of all the charges against him, and there was further sign of relaxing attitudes when, in 1696, an Act was passed which allowed Quakers to affirm instead of taking the oath. This Act was a mixed blessing, for while on the one hand it relieved Friends, on the other it marginalised them, not allowing them to give evidence in criminal cases, to serve on juries or bear any office or place in government. The radical, confrontational movement of the 1650s and 60s was being domesticated and isolated, and this is reflected in the reaction of Chichester Meeting to the Lucas bequest. The young George Fox might well have found some dynamic way to use the money - to establish a new meeting in a place where there was none perhaps - but by the 1690s, after years of difficulties, fines and imprisonments local Friends were not so adventurous and settled on a new building for the existing Meeting.

Matters did not move fast. It was five years later in 1698 that the Monthly Meeting discussed the possession and repair of the Hornet building, which had been purchased only ten years before. It was reported to be in a very dilapidated state, partly perhaps because of the attacks in '83, (when Friends were only renting it) though it must also be remembered that at this period most buildings were constructed of timber, with little or no foundation, and it was typical for such structures to need constant repair and renewal. In August 1698 Monthly Meeting decided to sell. However there was a difficulty, for by this time John Martin, who had a share in the freehold, had also died. His heir was the thirteen year old Josiah whose articles of apprenticeship had been paid by Quarterly Meeting at considerable expense eight months earlier. When it was discovered that he was also receiving an income from Friends in the form of interest on his share in the Meeting House there were second thoughts. It was felt that he should pay some of his apprenticeship himself and negotiations were started with his grandfather, Nicholas Rickman, acting as his guardian.

The matter was resolved by December when Quarterly Meeting finally approved the sale, but the following March (1699) it was reported that, though some progress had been made with both the sale and the finding of a new site, neither matter "was yet perfected". This was perhaps a good thing for the money from the Lucas will had still not been received. In June 1699 it was reported that there was prospect of payment. It was not in fact until December that John Hammond and James Steel were able to inform the meeting that they had at last obtained it.

By April 1700 a site had been found, a piece of ground which may have previously housed a cockpit. It was in Priory Street (sic) and surrounded on three sides by the land of Cockpit House, today known as Friars' Gate. It was a quiet corner: the street ended then at the city walls which were still complete at this point (a breach was made and the street extended in the nineteenth century). Opposite sheep were grazed in the big field belonging to the Duke of Richmond. Monthly Meeting met on 2nd April and members present, including Richard Green the Birdham blacksmith, gave consent to Hammond and Steel to "bargen and by (this) peace of ground in order to build a meeting house in Chichester." In June it is reported that the old meeting house had been sold (for fifty four pounds) and finally, by 7th November 1700, that the new one was completed. It was a plain wainscoted room with two large sash windows and a raised bench for the elders. After the attacks seventeen years before the building was designed for security with no ground floor windows onto the street, though there were two on the first floor to serve as look-outs if necessary. The yard was protected by a high wall and a stout door through which any marauder would have to pass before passing a second door into the meeting room. Happily these precautions were never needed: the

The exterior of the meeting house changed little from when it was built in 1700 until the taking of this picture in 1965.

years of violence had ended and the new building knew only tranquillity.

Meanwhile, on the other side of the Atlantic, the Meeting in Chichester Pennsylvania was also prospering and the first, timber built, meeting house was erected in 1703, just three years after that in Priory Road.

3: Sobriety and Good Works 1700:1908

The year 1700 was a turning point for Friends in many different ways. The generational change was marked again when Richard Green died in 1702. William Penn was also growing old – he left Warminghurst in 1707 and retired to Buckinghamshire.

Another change was in the social composition of the group. In the early years Friends were drawn from a wide spectrum of society including people like Penn, whose father was an admiral and a courtier. However the repression which started with Clarendon had its effect: men of substance did not give up their faith but their sons and heirs did not usually follow them. With the restoration of the monarchy times were different, believers were often imprisoned merely for attending meetings, and those that were not could expect to be heavily penalised for the non-payment of tithes. For wealthy young men with a lot to lose it was a daunting prospect. On the other hand the aspiring poor did continue to join: they had less to lose in terms of personal wealth and more to gain in terms of mutual support. By 1700 the social composition of the group had become much more humble but from then on honesty, hard work and the aforesaid mutual support helped members to better themselves and move up the social scale.

Humility and aspiration make men law-abiding. There were no fresh challenges to convention like those of the early radicals, which had so often led to dire punishment. Quakers still affirmed, used the thee/thou and refused to doff their hats, but these things had become tolerated as religious eccentricities. As early as 1683, when two London Friends went to plead the Quaker case with the King, they reported that a courtier "gently removed our hats". As if to emphasise their new role as harmless misfits, Friends adopted a sort of uniform (Quaker dress) in the early years of the new century. It was as unthreatening a testimony as the monk's habit.

Another change at this point was the emergence of social work programmes: Bristol Meeting started a job creation scheme and school in 1696, London started a similar programme in 1702, though it was the school that prospered and lives on today as the Friends' School at Saffron Walden. Chichester was not so ambitious but did help a steady stream of individuals, sometimes very substantially as in the case of Ann Roberts who was paid an allowance sufficient to live on, or Josiah Martin, the orphan boy apprenticed in 1698. Another individual helped was John Palmer who lived for several years rent free in the room above the meeting house. In 1737 there was some irritation that he had taken a house closer to town yet had not cleared his goods. He was given notice to clear his room and deliver the key by Michaelmas or pay fifty shillings a year rent. He was still there twelve months later, claiming that a well was needed, which wasn't deemed reasonable. He finally left the following year.

One of the reasons for the length of this dispute may have been Quaker decision making. Then as now meetings had to be called, and the "sense of the meeting" had to be discerned, a simple majority was not enough. This was a matter of principle - what was important was to gain the truth not a majority in a vote. This remains an unusual idea in Western societies where virtually all decision making, in the courts or Parliament for example, is adversarial. The Quaker way is not and this can be time consuming.

John Palmer was not the only person to leave: membership was falling throughout the country, a tendency which Friends shared with Baptists, Presbyterians and Independents during the whole of the eighteenth and early nineteenth centuries. A major cause of decline for Quakers at this time was the dismissal of members who married out.

Under external pressures they had become much less open minded than in the early years. Excluded from mainstream society they supported each other in very real and practical ways, providing the sort of benefits today given by the State, but in return the Meeting felt entitled to exercise great control over members' lives. The case of James Grace in Chichester is typical. He was married by a priest to a woman not a Friend. Members appointed by the Meeting, visited him and expressed their concern but did not feel he was taking the matter seriously enough. He was formally disowned by the Society in December 1769, but there were expressions of sorrow and hope of his repentance. Others suffered the same fate for marrying out while at least one did not marry at all - Sarah Chandler, a servant, was disowned for committing fornication. Affairs of the heart were not responsible for all dismissals - a man called Dalby was read out of the Meeting for the 'disgraceful treatment' of his brother, but exactly what he had done is not recorded. Sometimes matters were settled less drastically - Inigo Chipper for example made a written confession in the minute book and expressed his sorrow. He had got disgracefully drunk "as is my nature" and then picked a fight. He stayed a member.

Stern discipline and legal discrimination both combined to reduce membership. As early as 1737 the Petworth, Steyning and Birdham Meetings of the Chichester Monthly Meeting had closed, and the decline continued throughout the century. In 1822 the Chichester and Lewes Monthly Meetings amalgamated but had only three congregations between them: Chichester, Brighton and Lewes.

Perhaps one of the reasons for Chichester's continuance was its ownership of the meeting house. Moreover a trust deed had been drawn up in 1768 stipulating that it and the graveyards be used as such for ever. There could never thereafter be any question of selling them and putting the proceeds to different purpose. It was at almost exactly this time that Thomas Walls, the owner of the adjoining house (Friars' Gate), did some very extensive remodelling, giving it a Georgian facade. It is possible the trust deed was drawn up as the result of a bid to purchase the meeting house and enlarge the Friars' Gate garden.

At this time there was a challenge of a different kind for American

Friends: the timber built meeting house in Chichester Pennsylvania burnt down but was quickly replaced by the stone building which still stands and is now on the US National Register of Historic Places. The great-great grandparents of President Abraham Lincoln were members and there are probably several of his ancestors in the graveyard.

Chichester Meeting House Pennsylvania, rebuilt 1769,
Still in occasional use by Friends

In Britain while the eighteenth century was not a good period for the movement as a whole it was a time when many individual Friends enjoyed personal success. Inoculation against smallpox was developed by three Quakers; Coalbrookdale (a cradle of the industrial revolution) and the world's first iron bridge were built by Friends; Joseph Fry, a Bristol apothecary, founded the chocolate company. The Lloyd brothers could not go to Oxford like their father as the universities barred Dissenters, so they went into business and eventually founded the bank which bears their name. Barclays was started by descendants of Robert Barclay, while in Chichester James Hack and Charles Dendy founded the Chichester Bank in 1809 - it operated from premises in

East Street and prospered throughout the nineteenth century, eventually being incorporated with Barclays as a going concern. The present 1961 building has a plaque in the porch commemorating the Hack Dendy partnership.

Banking was not the only prosperous Quaker business in Chichester. James Hack's brother Stephen inherited the curriers (leather merchants) founded by his father, and in 1804 moved it into the extensive Little London premises now occupied by the City Museum. Stephen lived in the adjoining house (no. 30) which became a great centre of Quaker activity throughout the nineteenth century.

Friends' concern for social problems continued and developed. In 1772 slavery became an issue when John Woolman spoke at the Yearly Meeting greatly raising awareness. Three petitions organized by Friends were sent to Parliament in the following years, and the first anti-slavery Bill was passed in 1807 with strong support from the Society, though Quakers were still excluded from Parliament and had to rely on the MP William Wilberforce, not a Friend, to promote it.

Elizabeth Fry began her prison reform work in Newgate a few years later, establishing a school there, in 1817, for the children of the inmates. She was an inveterate campaigner and had visited Chichester in November 1816 as a guest of the Hacks. She was "poorly" the whole time but there were, never-the-less, two "well attended and very satisfactory public meetings". The Newgate school was in a tradition of Quaker education. In 1779 a new school was started at Ackworth, in Yorkshire, for boarding children "whose parents are not in affluence". Chichester Monthly Meeting was asked to support the venture with a subscription in 1805. In America the Meeting in Chichester Pennsylvania founded a grammar school in 1793. A most significant educational venture in Britain was the foundation by the Quaker Joseph Lancaster, in 1801, of Borough Road, a free London day school. It attracted great attention, George III subscribed, and its success led to the foundation of The British and Foreign School Society, a formative influence in the development of state education.

Joseph Lancaster visited Chichester on 13th September 1810 at the invitation of the local Quakers John Barton and John Marsh. He spoke

Stephen Hack's workshop in Little London,
is now the District Museum.
The adjoining house was his home and
John Barton a frequent visitor.
The premises were later occupied by:
John Hack (Adelaide)
Thomas Smith (Mayor 1865)
and William Smith (six times Mayor).

in the Assembly Rooms about his monitorial system, which basically consisted of a teacher drilling older pupils who then drilled younger ones, allowing one adult to instruct very large numbers of children. Following Lancaster's visit committees were formed, subscription lists opened and by 1812 two schools were established. John Barton was deeply involved and sat on both the boys' and the girls' committees, only resigning in 1850, two years before his death. His brother in law, Stephen Hack of the Chichester Bank family, also served and other Quakers feature in the subscription lists. The schools were non-sectarian, and though Friends took a leading role in their establishment and management, the vast majority of the pupils were from the C of E. When the state system finally absorbed the two secondary schools they were allowed to keep the name Lancastrian until late in the twentieth century. The name still lives on at the Lancastrian Infants' School.

John Barton was an economist of some repute, Ricardo, Malthus and John Stuart Mill all refer to his thesis on the Influence of Machinery on Labour. The London School of Economics has some of his manuscripts to this day. He was well known in Chichester both as a businessman and a man of letters. The Lancastrian Schools were not his only interest in education. In 1825 he was one of the original promoters of the Mechanics' Institute and "for many years he lectured within its walls in an able and popular manner". He remained treasurer of the Institute until it merged with the Literary and Philosophical Society and the new joint institution moved into the splendid new building it had constructed, and which still stands at 45 South Street.

The reputation of Quakers at the beginning of the nineteenth century was quite different from that of the early days. They were no longer seen as surly and possibly dangerous radicals, but rather as a sober and disciplined people given to good works and worthy of respect. In 1814, for example, the then Tsar, Alexander I, made a progress along the south coast of England and almost certainly passed through Chichester. At Portsmouth he had expressed the wish to visit a family of Quakers and a house had been suggested. There was such a crowd when he arrived that the plan was abandoned. However a few miles further on he saw a family in their Quaker dress standing at their gate. The coach was stopped and the royal party descended, most courteously introduced themselves and went in to take refreshment. They asked about the Meeting, were friendly with the children and after a short stay bade an affectionate farewell. The family were called Rickman and may have been descendants of the Nicholas Rickman so badly treated by the Chichester gaoler in 1662, grandfather to Josiah Martin the orphan boy apprenticed 1698.

The growing esteem in which Friends were held led to new self confidence in public life. By 1820 John Barton felt able to vigorously (verbally) attack the Chichester MP, William Huskisson, at an election meeting in the Assembly Rooms. He received great applause – somewhat to the alarm of his brother in law, the banker James Hack, who perhaps feared reprisals. There were none - and a few years later the esteem in which Friends were held nationally was reflected in the law. The Test and Corporation Acts were finally repealed in 1828. Quakers at last enjoyed full civil liberty.

About this time the Hacks made enquiries of the Quakers in York asking about a young man, Thomas Smith, whom they wanted to take on as a business partner. The ability of Friends to contact reliable people in all parts of the country was an important element in their business successes. In buchaneering times the network of trustworthy men and women who belonged to the Society, and who could always be called upon as fellow Friends, was a valuable asset.

Smith must have received the endorsement of the Quakers in York for he duly became a partner. A few years later, when John Hack was advised by his doctor to seek a better climate, it was to the Smiths that he sold the business. He then sailed with his family for South Australia, just established as a Crown Colony, and at the time spoken of by Friends as the "Pennsylvania of the South".

The family arrived in 1837 and Hack rapidly became an influential figure in the establishment of the new town of Adelaide. He was the first government contractor, a friend of the Governor, served on numerous committees and named some of the streets, among them Barton terrace honouring his uncle and Sussex Street his home county. Pennington (sic) Terrace, probably named after the Quaker theologian

Isaac Penington, was the site of the 1840 meeting house. The land was given by Hack but the building by the London Yearly Meeting which shipped it out, prefabricated, from England. It is still in use, the oldest place of worship in Adelaide and now on the official Australian heritage list. Today it is entirely surrounded by the buildings of the Anglican Cathedral so as Friends sit quietly on Sunday mornings they can hear the sound of their neighbors' hymn-singing.

Adelaide Meeting House 1840, still home to the Adelaide Meeting

John Hack's early success is reminiscent of that of William Clayton in Pennsylvania a hundred and fifty years earlier. Quaker emigrants tended to do well, they were responsible and hard working. They were also, from Quaker business meetings, in which all members take part, very familiar with the process of making group decisions: it is not surprising that both men became involved in government. There is a sad end however to the Quaker connection with John Hack - a great collapse in property values in the 1840s made him bankrupt and owing large sums to at least one other member of the Meeting. He left the Society of Friends at this time, perhaps finding it easier to make a new start in fresh company. Friends appear to have dealt kindly with him, he himself offered no explanation for the resignation. The family became Methodists. Back in England Hack's old house at Graylingwell Farm, where he had lived when first married, was occupied by another Quaker family, the Sewells, whose daughter Anna was later to become famous as the author of the children's classic "Black Beauty".

In Britain the nineteenth century was important for Friends in various ways: slavery was finally ended in 1838 after an Act in 1833; the first Friend took his seat in Parliament; George Cadbury and Joseph Rowntree established their famous businesses. Both were model employers: Cadbury built Bournville, a garden suburb, for his workers and the Rowntree family was responsible for the social research trust which bears their name. Many years later Seebohm Rowntree was to play an important part in the genesis of the first National Insurance Act, Churchill and Lloyd George both acknowledging his influence. In Chichester the two Lancastrian schools were a real achievement, albeit not by Friends alone. Some members supplied the first lifeboat at Selsey in the middle years of the century. It was called 'The Friends', cost £180, and rescued seven men in 1864. After five years it was moved from Selsey as too large - lifeboats were rowed in those days - but it served a further nineteen years elsewhere, saving another fifty five lives.

An important development in mid-century (1861) was that Quaker dress and Quaker speech (thee/thou) were no longer insisted upon as essential for those undertaking service for the Society, and both quickly dropped out of fashion. A service which was to become widespread shortly after was the Adult School Movement which, though most of the teaching was on Sunday, bore little relation to the Sunday Schools of today, being a literacy programme for men and women of all ages. It was through this movement that a young Anglo-German came to know Friends. He left Germany to avoid army service and, as a pacifist and a befriended traveller, his story was typical of

Quakers who had always tended to pacifism and internationalism. The young man's name was Charles Hess and he had three daughters who were, many years later, to become valued members in Chichester.

Throughout the latter part of the nineteenth century the Chichester Meeting continued its decline, a number of the younger and more dynamic Friends had left for South Australia to join John Hack and by 1851 there were only an average of fourteen left worshipping on Sundays. By 1870 the total membership was thirteen, all of one family, the Smiths. Thomas Smith was the man who had come to Chichester in the 1820s to partner John Hack in the curriers. Like many of the newly enfranchised non-conformists of the day Thomas took a leading part in public life, he was an ardent Liberal and rose to become Mayor in 1865. There weren't many Quakers but the few who remained were people of influence.

Photo courtesy of Chichester District Museum

William Smith reads the Jubilee Proclamation at the Cross

William Smith, son of Thomas, was even more important in the civic life of Chichester – he too was elected Mayor, in 1886, and the

West Sussex Gazette recorded that he affirmed rather than take the Oath "being one of those people called Quakers". In 1887 he was Mayor again and took a prominent part in Queen Victoria's Jubilee celebrations amongst other things planting the first memorial tree in Jubilee Park. His father died three years later at the age of ninety two and was the last person to be buried at Priory Road.

In all William served as Mayor six times, transferred the water works to the City Corporation, was the original promoter of the town drainage system, a Justice of the Peace, an Alderman of Chichester and Alderman of West Sussex County Council from its inception. He was made a Freeman of Chichester in 1905, one of only twenty three individuals in the twentieth century to be so honoured.

William continued to worship at Priory Road, but he was often alone in the simple, elegant, old room where so many had sat before. At some periods meetings were held in the afternoon when the western sun would have slanted in on him through the sash windows which looked onto the graveyard and the trees of the Friars' Gate garden. In 1908, an elderly man and not in the best of health, he left the town to live with his family in Rustington, and the meeting house closed.

In a curious parallel development the Chichester Pennsylvania Meeting had so diminished that it also closed, in 1910, its members becoming part of the nearby Concord Meeting.

4: War and Pacifism 1908:1967

The Priory Road building remained closed for seventeen tumultuous years. The Great War started in 1914 and Friends became very unpopular because of their pacifism. Conscription was introduced and conscientious objectors imprisoned. In 1916 some were sent to France in order that they might, under the different regulations obtaining there, be shot as deserters, though the policy was reversed before any actual executions took place. Friends in Parliament were, with the Independent Labour members, instrumental in the introduction of a "conscience clause" to the Conscription Act. Many Quakers served in medical units and the young men of the Friends Ambulance Unit eventually gained considerable respect for their courage and care.

There was no Meeting in Chichester during these troubled times but one started again in 1925. William Hobson, a worker in one of the Quaker Adult Schools, had come to live in the neighbourhood and with his help Priory Road was reopened in the summer for two Sundays each month. In winter it opened on only one Sunday a month, there being fewer holiday makers to swell the gathering. A Monthly (administrative) Meeting was held at the Meeting House in 1928 but by February 1930 it was closed again, probably because of the cold and dark in winter. However meetings were being held, presumably in private houses, and a committee was appointed by the Monthly Meeting to discuss the situation with local Friends. One of the committee members was Ronald Littleboy, whose brother Wilfred was Clerk to the Yearly Meeting. As a young man Wilfred had re-established the Australian connection when he visited Adelaide in 1909, running some very memorable Young Friends' Camps. Eleanor Littleboy, the niece of Ronald and Wilfred, was many years later to become Convener to the Elders in Chichester. The 'Elders' have a special responsibility for the spiritual life of the community.

The upshot of the 1930 discussions was that internal repairs were undertaken, at a cost of over sixteen pounds, and the following year a further seven pounds was spent on the installation of gas lighting, but despite this, in November 1931, meetings were discontinued "for the winter months". They were not to reopen for another ten years.

The problem at this time was that of a very thin spread of people over a very wide area, and the people in question were mainly reliant on public transport. Friends were not evangelical and did not build up a base of local support.

One matter achieved before the 1931 closure was that the Hornet burial ground finally became a Quaker freehold. The Corporation wished to take some of the land for road widening and initiated negotiations which led to the legal change - the four pence annual rent not having been paid since 1699. A strip of the newly acquired land was dedicated to the public for the new pavement and the rest was let to the Corporation, as a public garden.

The 1930s were a troubling decade. The autocratic militaristic regimes in Germany and Japan represented the antithesis of Quaker beliefs. Hitler came to power in 1933 and the first refugees began to arrive here. Dr Peter Aris, a judge who had spoken against the Nazis, arrived penniless and was befriended by Friends in Cambridge for whom he formed a deep respect. His daughter, Jan Tregear, became a member of the Chichester Meeting thirty years later.

However at the time of Aris's arrival in Cambridge the Meeting House in Chichester stood largely unused, though there was a caretaker living in the upstairs room, an elderly woman called Emma Bazeley. In 1935 the Christian Alliance cancelled a meeting they had been planning, as they felt it would be detrimental to her health. (Their concern may have been justified - she died the following year.) Other tenants included the NUR, and the Chichester Christian Spiritualist Church, which rented the building in November 1939 for two years. They did not have exclusive use however, for in July 1940 twenty one Quakers from around the district gathered for a special afternoon meeting - Worthing Friends reported that they "had fellowship and a good social time". Six months later Chichester was recognized as "allowed", and once again there were regular Quaker meetings in Priory Road, under the care of Worthing. When the arrangement with the Spiritualists ended, in 1941, it was decided not to let them stay longer as Friends required the building themselves.

The Second World War, 1939-1945, posed fresh challenges. There was not the jingoism of the First War but there were grave shortages, floods of refugees, many killed and injured and much need for reconciliation. A typical story concerns a German Jew who had fled to Britain with his young family. In 1946 he returned to his homeland, and it was Friends who broke to him the news of the death of his parents on their way to Auschwitz. They also encouraged him to visit his non-Jewish mother-in-law and make his peace with her, which he did - and the family was reconciled by his generosity of spirit. His daughter later became a member at Chichester and has written a book

After the meeting: outside the old Priory Road meeting house 1947

The old meeting room, probably unchanged from 1700

recording the memories of some of the Jewish and mixed-race refugee children of the time. She writes of her father's experience with the Quakers, and of their advice to him. Friends so distinguished themselves in reconciliation and refugee work after the war, that they were awarded the 1947 Nobel Peace Prize.

In the July of the same year Chichester once again became a Particular Meeting and a Monthly (regional administrative) Meeting was held in the city, the first for nineteen years and only the second in the century. The first Particular Meeting began its business by minuting thanks to Worthing for their oversight and, on a more practical level, to the two Friends who had installed electric lighting.

Other early minutes record wider concerns, particularly for peace. The leaflet "Atomic Power a Quaker Reply" was sent to thirty six local clergy together with a protest about conscription. There was a more public testimony in October 1947 when a letter from the Clerk was published in the Chichester Observer. "Members of the Society of Friends deeply deplore the remarks of the Dean of Chichester in his recent Battle of Britain address which can only intensify the prevailing atmosphere of distrust and despair and hinder the work of the United Nations Organisation and all who seek to promote international goodwill." The new Particular Meeting was starting with a radical challenge to the establishment reminiscent of Fox himself.

Food parcels were still being received from America in 1947 and the Meeting helped with their allocation. However it was a sign of the times that it also decided to send a monthly parcel to the Russian Zone in Germany. There were other German connections: two German POWs visited Priory Road and one later wrote to the Meeting which duly minuted its pleasure that "Hans Netz is back with his family". Chichester was not the only Meeting concerned about food and hunger at this time: in Oxford it was very largely Friends who founded the "Oxford Committee for Famine Relief" now known as "Oxfam".

There were also domestic concerns: as the forties ended these were about the state of the Priory Road building. The gable bulged ominously and furniture beetle was active. An architect was called in - Hubert Lidbetter who had designed the award winning Friends' House in Euston Road. He recommended the upper part of the gable be rebuilt, a major job which was duly done, and a contemporary minute adds that the builders "also distempered the china cupboard". In 1950 it was decided to defer improvements to the outbuildings but note that they might become necessary later.

THE DEAN'S BATTLE OF BRITAIN ADDRESS observer 11.10.47

[*To the Editor*]

SIR,—It is the experience of the Society of Friends that human security can only be obtained through harmony and goodwill among men and nations. Harmony cannot be fostered by the apparatus of discord, nor goodwill cherished by the equipment of hate.

Members of the Society of Friends in Chichester therefore deeply deplore the remarks of the Dean of Chichester in his recent " Battle of Britain " address, which can only intensify the prevailing atmosphere of distrust and despair ; and hinder the work of the United Nations Organisation and all who seek to promote international goodwill.

Yours, etc.,

Chichester Preparative Meeting of the Society of Friends,

GODFREY C. MACE,
Clerk.

Chichester Observer 11th October 1947

Another problem was that of attendance - the Meeting was still very small and thin-spread over a wide area. In 1949 consideration was given to meeting twice a month only, which was not felt to be a good idea, but Littlehampton members were encouraged to gather occasionally in their own district. Two years later when Littlehampton was recognized as "allowed", another group started to meet occasionally in Bognor Regis. This fragmentation further reduced the numbers in Chichester and in 1951 it was decided to form a new joint Chichester and Bognor Particular Meeting, with meetings for worship alternating between the towns.

During the whole of this period the Christian Spiritualists had continued to share the building, the earlier decision not to renew their lease having been reversed. The War had made difficulties in finding accommodation and Friends doubtless felt they should share theirs. There were some problems, notably when the Spiritualists erected a large exterior notice board against the express wishes of Friends. It featured a cross: Quakers have no symbols and no rituals in their plain meeting rooms, so this was unwelcome and quickly removed. A year or two later, in 1955, the Spiritualists left Priory Road.

Attendance there was growing again, and in 1957 it was decided to open weekly which proved a great success. Towards the end of 1957 Chichester became a Particular Meeting once more, with Bognor "allowed" under its care. In 1958 Bognor too started to meet every Sunday. Since its fresh start in the dark days of the war Chichester had spawned two new meetings and was growing strongly.

Facilities at the meeting house were not good. There was no central heating, the lavatory was outdoors and access to the upstairs room was by a steep winding stair. In 1962 Friends decided on a programme of modest improvements - new toilet facilities, renovation of the upstairs room, and a fitted sink in the tearoom. The projected cost was just over five hundred pounds and the subject was raised with the Monthly Meeting whose trustees were (and still are) the legal owners. They were ready to make funds available, but called for a bolder and more imaginative scheme and new plans were prepared. Finally, after a year of discussion, the architect sought planning permission from the City Council - and was refused. Ironically the builders' estimate for the work arrived a week or two later. This second, bolder, plan would have cost three thousand pounds had the Council given permission.

A modified plan was submitted to the City shortly after. Before reaching a decision it asked the advice of the Area Planning Officer who made his position plain. "This is quite acceptable as was the first application. It's this sort of idiotic decision by the City, amounting egmerely with interference with the detailing of a perfectly competent architect, that brings design control into disregard". Despite this endorsement the second application was also turned down. The Friends' architect discussed the scheme very thoroughly with the City Planners and made a number of changes before submitting a third application. In June 1964 planning permission was finally obtained but there was a new difficulty, as Monthly Meeting thought the City was being unreasonable and decided not to approve the plan agreed by the architect and the Council. The City Planning Committee then turned down three further schemes, despite their having the support of a local Councillor and the Deputy City Surveyor. In January 1965 it was decided to appeal to the Ministry of Housing and Counsel was briefed. In February the Bishop came to hear of the problem and asked to be put in touch with a local Friend who could show him the premises and explain the situation.

During this period the Meeting was expanding fast. In March 1965 Sunday worship was changed from afternoon to morning and this resulted in a much larger attendance. There were also more children, not least those of the Tregears, who had three. Jan Aris, the daughter of the refugee judge, had married David Tregear, a young solicitor who had been a conscientious objector, and the young family had come to live locally.

Two other members at this time were Leslie and Harriet Metcalf. Leslie was a distinguished engineer who had worked in Russia in the twenties and who, for many cold-war years, chaired the East/West Relations Committee of the Friends' Yearly Meeting. On retiring from his engineering job he and his wife set up home in Chichester before, in the summer of 1965, going to serve for a time as volunteer wardens of the Vienna Quaker House. There he played an important role in organizing the "Pugwash" conferences, informal meetings of diplomats from East and West, on a strictly private basis, in order that they might get to know each other as people.

Shortly after the departure of Leslie Metcalf the Appeal against refusal of planning permission was withdrawn as it had become clear that an altogether bigger building was needed for the rapidly growing Meeting and the plan under appeal would not have given sufficient accommodation. In April 1966, after yet more thought, an application was submitted for an entirely new building. Once again memos flowed between the City Council and the Area Planners, who were enthusiastic: "The proposal is very good indeed architecturally, a most sympathetic scheme with good materials." A month later this seventh planning application was given consent. The estimated cost was thirteen thousand pounds, considerably more than the five hundred first envisaged in 1962, albeit for a far more modest scheme.

Not everyone agreed about the architectural merits of the new building. In June 1966 a bitter letter was received from Basil Shipham, owner of the adjoining Friars' Gate House, who thought the proposal "quite horrible". Friends worked hard in drafting a suitable reply, gently pointing out that they had visited and consulted him on a number of occasions and that the plan had gained wide approval in the City. They earnestly hoped he would find his forebodings unjustified. Twelve months later, when the new building was under construction, Mr Shipham wrote indignantly to the Chichester Observer, expressing disgust and surprise that planning consent had ever been given. As a Freeman of the City he had perhaps expected to be able to forestall the grant of permission - and indeed his influence might be an explanation for the repeated difficulties which Friends suffered before getting it. The story was the front page lead in the paper, under the banner headline: "J.P. angered by Quakers' new building".

Construction began in February 1967. The builder was Robert Heasman, the Friend who had conceived the final design, and who was so involved with the job that his workmen, teasing, said he polished every brick. His wife, Iris, had joined the Meeting soon after it restarted in the early forties, was Clerk for many years and later became its longest standing member. The new building was formally opened on a Saturday afternoon in November 1967. The Mayor was present, together with the principals of the higher-education colleges and representatives of all the local churches. Three hundred and twenty years had softened attitudes from the days when George Fox insulted the Justices and interrupted the Baptists.

Friends occupied their new meeting room that day with the Meeting itself healthy and growing. The room was on the exact site of the earlier one, so they sat on the same spot, if not within the same walls, as their forebears. The speaker was Ormorod Greenwood, an ex-BBC producer, whose message was something of a surprise: "What is this place for?" he asked. "A few people will sit in silence together and from time to time someone will say something which usually won't amount to much except a few platitudes or anecdotes. Occasionally there will be a fund raising activity, a sale of work, a concert or a dramatic performance. It is a traditional programme, an inadequate programme, a lop sided programme in a desperate world."

The audience that Saturday afternoon got a real challenge on a day when many would have expected comfortable congratulations. Perhaps that was in itself appropriate: Friends, while generally pacifists, have had a history of stating and facing uncomfortable truths from the time of the outspoken George Fox. The new building was opened in an appropriate way: the Quakers in Chichester started a new phase in their ongoing story in typically Quaker fashion.

The next day they gathered for worship, as they did every Sunday. As Friends sat in their new meeting room, celebrating an old tradition of quiet assembly, they no doubt thought about the words of the day before. Perhaps they also remembered the words of Robert Barclay, the early thinker who had joined Fox and Penn at Warminghurst in 1677. "For when I came into the silent assemblies of God's people" he wrote "I felt a secret power among them which touched my heart." Over the years the Chichester Meeting had been sustained, sometimes at great cost, by generations of men and women who on the one hand were ready to state and face and act upon uncomfortable truths, and who on the other hand shared Barclay's perception of the silent assemblies which lie at the heart of Quaker experience.

Afterword

The Quakers still meet in Chichester, Littlehampton, Bognor and Adelaide, all of which are now Preparative Meetings. There is a small "allowed" Meeting, under the care of Chichester, in Midhurst. Friends in Upper Chichester Pennsylvania are now members of Concord Meeting, though the old Upper Chichester Meeting House is still used for worship twice a year.

Chichester Friends' Meeting, Priory Road. *Sundays at 10.45am*
Littlehampton Friends' Meeting, 23 Church Street. *Sundays at 10.30am*
Bognor Friends' Meeting, 6 Victoria Drive. *Sundays at 10.30am*
Adelaide Friends' Meeting, 40a Pennington Terrace, North Adelaide, South Australia. *Sundays at 11am*
Midhurst Friends' Meeting, Midhurst Grammar School, North Street. *Second and fourth Sundays at 10.30am*
Chichester Friends' Meeting, 611 Meeting House Road, Boothwyn Pennsylvania USA. *Third Sundays in April and September at 3pm*

Despite their unevangelical nature Friends always welcome visitors

BOOKS AND SOURCES

A Brief History of Upper Chichester	Township UC	Township of Upper C.
Chichester a Documentary History	R R Morgan	Phillimore
Chichester Friends' Meeting	R Pyle Davis	Concord MM, PA USA
Emperor Alexander I in Sussex	A Bissel	Fr Hist Soc 49/5 1961
English Historical Documents VIII	Ed: D Douglas	Eyre & Spottiswoode
George Fox and the Children of Light	J Fryer	Kyle Cathie
John Barton Hack A Quaker Pioneer	Geo Morphett	Pioneers' Assoc of SA
Joseph Lancaster: Poor Child's Friend	Joyce Taylor	Campanile Press
Journal of George Fox (ed J Nickalls)	George Fox	London YM
King Charles II	A Fraser	Mandarin
Lawmaking and Legislators in PA	C Horle et al	University of PA
Oxford Companion to British History	Ed: J Cannon	Oxford
Quakerism and the Social Structure	R Vann	Past & Present 43 1969
Reformation and Revolution	R Ashton	Paladin
Sussex Martyrs	E Stoneham	Sussex Martyrs Com
The Illustrated Pepys	R Latham	Bell and Hyman
The Lancastrian School for Girls	Grace Hine	Chi City Council
The Leaves Have Lost Their Trees	D Darke	Sessions of York
The Millionth Snowflake	C Stevenson	Adelaide Meeting
The Quakers: Money and Morals	James Walvin	John Murray
The Story of Quakerism	E Vipont	Bannisdale Press
Then and Now: Baptists in Chichester	P Thatcher	Chi Baptist Church
William Penn	Thakeham	Praxis
William Penn in West Sussex	Martin O'Neill	WSCC

Pre-1900 minutes and other records of the Arundel and Chichester Monthly Meeting and the Arundel and Lewes Monthly Meeting are deposited in the East Sussex Record Office in Lewes. More recent minutes and Quaker records are stored in the strongroom of Brighton Meeting House. General local records, wills etc are from the West Sussex County Record Office. The Friends' House Library is an invaluable source of general Quaker information. Full notes for this paper are with the Preparative Meeting librarian. They can also be accessed on the internet at <chichesterquakers.org>

5th to 19th July 2000
10am – 5pm (not Sundays)

Quaker Tapestry Exhibition

Friends Meeting House Priory Road

Meetings from many countries have stitched panels about the life, work and history of The Society of Friends. The panels are normally on exhibition in Kendal but have travelled the country, most recently to Canterbury Cathedral. They are being exhibited in Chichester to celebrate the Tercentenary of the meeting in Priory Road.

Free admission Courtesy Coffee

Chichester City Museum
July 2000 (not Mondays)

Our Quaker Heritage

A special exhibition celebrating the history of Friends in Chichester

Guided walks: July 9th and 19th Lunchtime lecture: July 13th

TERCENTENARY CELEBRATIONS

Some of the events to mark 300 years in Priory Road

Saturday 22nd January 2000, 3-6 pm: Meeting House
A Three Hundredth Birthday Party for people of all ages!

Saturday 25th March 2000, 11am: Hornet Burial Ground
A Planting Ceremony to improve the Hornet Burial Ground.

Saturday 29th April to Wednesday 3rd May 2000
Trip to the '1652 Country' to celebrate our early history.

Tuesday 4th July 2000, 10am (all month): Museum
"Our Quaker Heritage" opens at the City Museum.

Wednesday 5th July 2000, 11am (till 19th): Meeting House
The Quaker Tapestry Exhibition opens

Friday 14th July 2000
American Friends arrive for a three to eight day stay.

Saturday 15th July 2000, 5pm and 7.30pm: Meeting House
'Talking Threads: Stories from the Quaker Tapestry' performed
by Barry and Jill Wilsher at the Meeting House

Tuesday 18th July 2000: Meeting House 7.30pm for 8pm
"A Tapestry of Friends" Harvey Gillman lecture

Saturday 23rd September to Wednesday 27th September 2000
Trip to the '1652 Country' to celebrate our early history.

Sunday 5th November 2000, 10.45am
Special Meeting for Worship with invited guests. The original meeting house
was licensed 7th day of 11th month 1700

1700 - 2000